STREETSCAPES

STREET

S C A P E S

MARTIN M. PEGLER

Retail Reporting Corporation, Inc.
New York

Retail Reporting Corporation
302 Fifth Avenue
New York, NY 10001

Distributors to the trade in the United States and Canada
Watson-Guptill Publishers
1515 Broadway
New York, NY 10036

Distributors outside the United States and Canada
Hearst Books International
1350 Avenue of the Americas
New York, NY 10019

Library of Congress Cataloging in Publication Data:
Retail Entertainment

Printed in Hong Kong
ISBN 0-934590-78-8

Designed by Dutton & Sherman

CONTENTS

INTRODUCTION

While it may take mountains, hills, lakes, streams and trees to create a landscape, it takes the mind and hands of man—and the man-made structures to arrange a streetscape. Some architects define a streetscape as a series of building facades designed and orchestrated, with variations, to affect a homogeneous look or setting. A streetscape may also be the texture and fabric of a street—a neighborhood—even a town or a city that may have taken decades or even centuries to "perfect." It can be a collection of structures of assorted styles and periods, gracefully patinaed and softened to create a unique and memorable look. More than just the buildings and structures, it is the signage, the graphics, the billboards, the display windows, the colors and lights and even the landscaping of the street. It is the composition of shapes and forms—of masses and details—of shadows and highlights: sometimes balanced and harmonious and sometimes kilter and at odds with itself. It is the building materials and the textures.

Streetscapes tell stories: stories about people, about a time in history, a place or a culture. These stories are rendered in brick and stone, in metal and wood. They recount how and where a people live: the places they live, eat and shop. A streetscape can also speak of where people escape to for a change from their everyday streetscape. Architects, designers, sculptors, painters, masons and metal molders contribute to the streetscape as do the graphic artists, sign painters and makers, neon blowers, lighting technicians, landscapers and gardeners.

In this book of Streetscapes we have combined many different streets formed over years of building and rebuilding as well as newly created "instant" neighborhoods of hotel/resort complexes, malls, and shopping and entertainment centers where the architects/designers have recreated another time and place to create the ambience.

This volume has been divided—quite arbitrarily—into several kinds of streetscapes. Arbitrarily because we have included in our section of "Old Towns" streets that are actually "Neighborhoods." That same Old Town street may also be a viable "Main Street" with shops and restaurants alive with activity. In some instances "Big Business" streetscapes could be as truthfully located in "Main Street." Barcelona is in "Old Town" but its designers shops are stocked with the newest and most fashion forward merchandise to be found on any "Main Street." Sedona's Tiaquepaque could just as well be a Mexican "Brigadoon": a town that has been a"asleep" for 100 years and has just been awakened as an arts and restaurant center. So, just enjoy strolling these streets culled from many countries and don't judge too harshly where we have placed them. Remember, a streetscape is not a "still life" but a live, kinetic, animated presentation of a place, a people, a time and a way of life

Martin M. Pegler

MAIN STREET

UNION SQUARE

SAN FRANCISCO, CA

An oasis, plunked down amid the department stores, specialty shops, hotels and commercial buildings, is Union Square, the heart of San Francisco and the major shopping area. Important shopping streets start out from here, the hub of the commercial city, and the square is highlighted with tall palm trees, shrubbery and plants. This plot of greenery sends its tentacles out towards other areas of this lovable, walkable city by the bay.

The names on the buildings may change, signs go up only to be replaced by others, but the streetscape remains the same: architecture as diverse as the citizens of the cosmopolitan city. Some famous department stores have disappeared—if in name only—but the buildings stand and flourish under new management.

Contrasting with the scale of the tall buildings are the intimate and colorful flower kiosks on the corner, the street vendors showing their wares, the pigeons that "own" the square and tolerate the gawking tourists and the trademark trolley that pulls itself up the first of many inclines.

Geart, Post, Powell and Stockton Streets border Union Square and here are housed many noted fashion boutiques.

POST AND GEARY STS.

SAN FRANCISCO, CA

These streets, running parallel to each other, start at Union Square and work their way down to Market Street. Here are housed some of the most advertised and promoted brand names in retail. The streetscape is lined with simple, handsome shopfronts—many with canopies of metal or canvas and sunscreens that create horizon-tal bands that cap the vertical architectural lines. They also keep the viewer's eye at street level and just above because the buildings that rise up are a melange of old and new, of classic and contemporary, of elegant and not so elegant. Age and San Francisco have blended them into a relaxed and comfortable streetscape that bespeaks of taste, of quality and of life as it is lived in San Francisco.

Awnings, canopies and skeletal marquees stretch out over the shopping street and invite shoppers into the high fashion stores below.

N.Y. / N.Y.

LAS VEGAS, NV

ARCHITECTS: GASKIN & BEZANSKI IN COLLABORATION WITH YATES-SILVERMAN

DESIGN CONCEPT: SIG ROGICH, PRIMADONNA RESORTS INC.

PHOTOGRAPHER: MMP/RVC

In the city that truly never sleeps and where bigger is better and the brightest is the best, every hotel/casino complex tries to outdo the other hotel/casino with bigger, bolder and more overwhelming images and scale.

N.Y./N.Y. is currently the "hottest" must-see sight in the sight-filled Las Vegas. The architectural concept of reproducing, in a reduced scale, dozens of noted NYC landmarks and facades is so staggering and so stupendous that this streetscape was reproduced on the front of the Arts & Leisure section of the auspicious New York Times.

According to Ada Louise Huxtable, the noted architecture critic and historian, "The real fake reaches its apogee in places like Las Vegas where it has been developed into an art form. Continuous, competitive frontages of moving lights and color and constantly accelerating novelty lead to the gaming tables and hotels. The purpose is clear and the solution is dazzling. The outrageous fake has developed its own indigenous style and lifestyle to become a real place. This is an urban design frontier where extraordinary things are happening."

Just take a stroll down Las Vegas Blvd. and you can sample the essence of a week of

N.Y. sightseeing. There are the famous sky-scrapers—the Empire State Building. And the Chrysler Bldg.—Radio City Music Hall, Grand Central Station, Ellis Island, Grant's Tomb, Soho, Little Italy—even a 300 ft. replica of the Brooklyn Bridge. Towering up front is the scaled down version of the Statue of Liberty. Spanning and spinning around this composition of towers and landmarks is a dare-devil roller coaster of bright red that ties all these N.Y. sights into a breath-taking, photo-snapping streetscape.

Though this isn't the "biggest" hotel/casino in Las Vegas, today it is the most talked about and most visited spot in town.

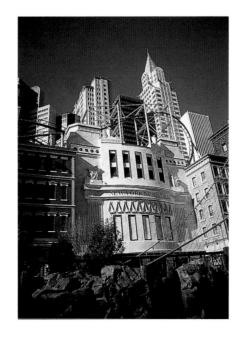

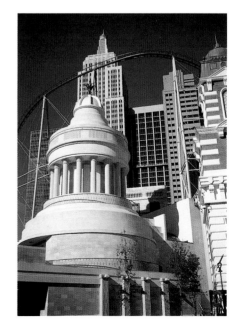

LAS VEGAS BLVD.

LAS VEGAS, NV

Besides the fabulous theme hotels that line this fanciful, heavily trafficked street in the fantasy town of Las Vegas, there are the retail shops and stores, the restaurants, the service and office buildings that are necessary parts of the city's life. As one strolls past N.Y./N.Y. there are wonders to behold such as the graphics and lighting explosion of the All Star Cafe's facade, the new M&M building decorated with colorful,

humungous M&Ms, and the four story high Coca Cola bottle that stands just a few feet away from it.

There is the heroic scaled Juke Box that frames the entrance to Country Star and further up the street the rising nose and periscope of the purple and yellow submarine that is "home" to Dive! Highly reflective glass and mirror faced facades add even more glitz, glimmer and shine to the already dazzling streetscape.

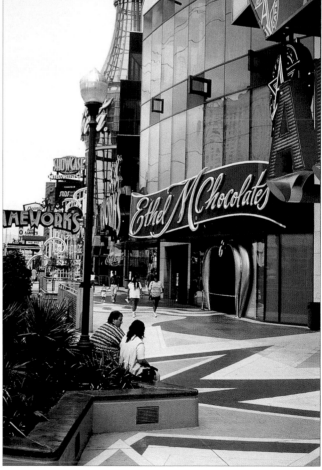

MILAN

It is difficult to award the envious title of "Fashion Capital" to any city today, but without a doubt, Milan must be a top contender on any fashion aware judge's list.

Milan has long been synonymous with smart, stylish, Italian couture and now—

more than ever—it holds firm to that recognition. In several parallel streets and just two or three crossing ones, are some of the most illustrious names in fashion: boutiques housed in classically inspired buildings built in the previous century of heavily coursed and textured stone and marble. The Italian

Renaissance heritage is evident and some of the "renovations" have been done with delicacy and loving concern for the architectural integrity of the street. The shopfronts, where "modernized," are simply and elegantly understated to coexist with the original buildings.

The texture is coarse vermicelli hammered stone and smooth slabs of stone laid in massive courses. All is gray, somber and only rarely relieved by an accent of greenery in a jardiniere out front. Where sleek marble has been applied, it either complements or continues the look of the architecture of the original.

The streetscape serves as the neutral background for the fashions exquisitely presented in the brilliantly illuminated, open-back show windows at street level.

RUE FRANCOISE PREMIER

PARIS, FRANCE

For over a century, Paris has been the fashion center of the world and though the fair city now has to share that title with other cities in Europe and around the world, it still remains synonymous with Haute Couture and names such as Chanel, Dior, Hermes, Cardin and Courreges.

Though the city is divided into arrondissements, certain streets in certain areas stand out like the Faubourg St. Honore, Rue Montaigne, Victor Hugo, Blvd St. Germain and the Rue Francoise. Though France has fought in several wars in the past 150 years, many of the handsome Beaux Arts buildings still stand as testimony to the city

planning genius of Baron Haussmann and the streetscapes designed in the mid 19th century. At street level there have been "face lifts"—usually considerate enough to maintain the look of the street and of the original architecture.

The Rue Francois is an excellent example of a top fashion street, home to many designer boutiques, that shows how times have subtly changed the street level vista of the street without affecting too much the genteel quality of the handsome old buildings that still make up the fashionable and fashion filled streetscape.

THE GRABEN

VIENNA, AUSTRIA

To many people, Vienna is the 19th century, the Blue Danube, wine, women and waltzes. However, like many major European cities, it is also a cultural and commercial center.

Starting at the Haas Haus (see entry) and heading down the Graben and into Kohimarkt and Karnterstrass, the streets are laden with shops selling fine jewelry, leather goods, designer ready-to-wear and other luxury items. Though the 19th century architecture dominates and the roof line is multi-leveled and decorated with a variety of ornate styles of the past, the street level

is contemporary—often avant garde with unique sculptural facades of marble, granite and fantasies of metal and glass.

The safe, sane and stolid look of the commercial architecture stands in sharp contrast to the freeform and fun attitude at street level that makes the Graben such a draw for local and visiting shoppers.

KURFURSTEIN

BERLIN, GERMANY

Long before the Wall came down, the main upscale and not so upscale shopping street in Berlin was Kurfursten–also know as Ku Damm. The wide thoroughfare cuts through the city and it is lined with trees, street plantings and stately and even more stately buildings that have withstood all forms of strife: political, cultural and retail.

Many of the handsome structures from the turn of the century stand as witnesses to what is happening today but the political and cultural upheavals of World War II have brought about changes including some rebuilding. Mixed in between the massive, rusticated stone buildings are newer glass and steel structures and renovated shopfronts that usually gently bridge the styles. Here are some of the shopfronts and facades found on the Ku Damm.

THE KO

DUSSELDORF, GERMANY

The main walking/shopping street of Dusseldorf is the Ko. The two sides of this fashion street are divided by a wide swath of greenery that is, itself interrupted by a stream of water. Small, metal balustraded bridges span the swan filled "lake" at the cross streets. Benches, trees, kiosks, and cafes fill the green space with a comfort and charm not usually found on main Fashion Streets.

The commercial structures on either side are highlighted with glass and metal canopies that extend out from the buildings to allow pedestrians to enjoy the changing display presentations in the windows below whether it rains or the sun shines.

Some of the boutiques and specialty stores personalize their presence on the street with topiary and flowering plants in planters set to either side of the store entrances.

UNIVERSAL CITYWALK

UNIVERSAL CITY, LOS ANGELES, CA

DESIGN: THE JERDE PARTNERSHIP, LOS ANGELES, CA

PHOTOGRAPHY: ANNETTE DEL ZOPPO, STEPHEN SIMPSON

"Citywalk is entertainment driven by reality," said the architect, Jon Jerde, the principal of The Jerde Partnership. The design firm was the main designer of Citywalk which is a two-street stretch of upscaled entertaining, reality suspended shops and dining experiences. Located in Universal City–just outside of Los Angeles–this wild, wacky and wonderfully exhilarating walk-

way connects the Universal Studio tour with the 6,000-seat amphitheater and the 18-screen movie complex.

In designing this always surprising and amusing, carnival-like streetscape, Jon Jerde took "L.A." as the theme. "The theme of L.A. is that there is no theme. That's what makes this city so eclectic. The style of Universal's Citywalk architecture pays homage to Los Angeles."

On this street you can expect to find a 1957 Chevy hurtling though space, a spaceship, 3-D pop-art murals, giant tinker toys, eagles soaring, heroic scaled crayons and color-color-color. Neon runs rampant—lights flash and flicker—there is shimmer and shine and the electricity that lights up the street is nothing compared to the excitement that is generated by the people that become part of the streetscape.

BEMBO

OHAMA, LIMA, PERU

DESIGN: JOSE A. ORREGA HERRERA, ARCHITECT, LIMA, PERU

Lima, the capital of Peru, is a city filled with brilliant color, a remarkably blue sky, verdant trees and stretches of grass, and flowers blazing in tropical colors—all man watered and nurtured in this rather dry city.

Bembo, a very popular fast food operation featuring hamburgers and fries, has free standing outlets all around the city. They

are readily recognized by the bright, primary color scheme and the highly original and exciting architecture designed by Jose Orrega Herrera of that city.

Using a vocabulary of simple geometric forms and shapes—accented with sharp diagonal fins or projecting canopies and softened with the fun use of circles and arcs, each Bembo is unique, distinctive and yet recognized as part of the fast food chain. On streets already looking like a child's drawing in crayon color hues, Bembo's red/yellow and blue coloration is demanding and distinctive.

SPORTS PLAZA & BOHEMIA

LIMA, PERU

DESIGN: JOSE A. ORREGA HERRERA

Adding highlights, bright colors, kinetic forms, startling shapes and exciting architecture to the already color saturated main streets of downtown Lima are these restaurants also designed by Jose A. Orrega Herrera.

Sr. Herrera has a sharp, contemporary architectural style that combines form and function with fun and fancy. His many designs are complemented by the striking high rise residences he has designed in the upscale San Isidro section of Lima. (see Neighborhoods, San Isidro.) Bohemia and Sports Plaza, shown on these pages, add special interest as well as an "attitude" to the downtown streetscape that is crammed with retail stores, other restaurants and commercial high-rise buildings.

MICHIGAN AVE.

CHICAGO, IL

The Million Dollar Mile—it really should be upped to Billion Dollar Mile—is a fabulous streetscape of early 20th century skyscrapers. It includes those housing newspaper empires that stand proudly just this side of the river that cuts through the downtown area of Chicago. Sleek contemporary facades and sweeping curves and arcs on the newer structures join the richly enhanced newspaper towers

along with the old Water Tower—a remnant of the last century and the Great Chicago Fire. This memorial to the past stands amid the new on a swath of greenery opposite one of the three vertical malls that line this major thoroughfare. The ultimate "exclamation point"—just before the street gives way to the Lake—is the soaring Hancock Building.

Up and down Michigan Ave. the street is lined with distinctive facades and store-

fronts such as Nike, Sony, Eddie Bauer, Neiman Marcus, Marshall Field and many other famous names in retailing. This is a changing streetscape, though the big buildings still frame the scene, at street level there is constant movement. One store moves out to make room for a bigger store—and each store seems to get bigger and more prominent than the one that was there before.

In addition to the high rising skyscrapers along Michigan Ave. there are the sweeps, arcs and curves that create welcoming entrances to the buildings. The twin circular towers make a definite impression of the Michigan Ave. Streetscape.

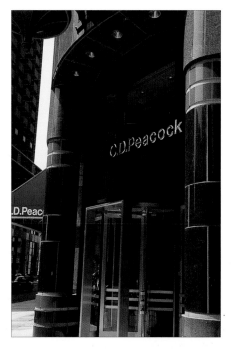

MICHIGAN AVE.

CHICAGO, IL

Michigan Ave. personifies American retailing today.

NEIGHBORHOODS

COVENT GARDEN / NEAL ST.

LONDON, ENGLAND

Though Liza Doolittle no longer sells her flowers outside of the opera house and the glass and iron open street structure is almost completely gone—replaced with a two-level shopping/dining/entertainment center—Covent Garden is perhaps now more than ever the meeting place for the young and the seekers of fun and entertainment. The Royal Opera House is still there to add some "class" as are some 19th century Georgian styled structures, but mostly the streets surrounding Covent Garden are filled with trendy fashion shops, tee shirt and souvenir stores and some upscaled fashion shops. There are also food shops for every taste.

Though the area is a crush of people on weekends, it is always full of tourists waiting to mix in with the locals. The architecture is a hodge podge of styles and periods, Classic and Georgian, quaint and period, or slick and contemporary, but somehow a patina seems to tone down the assorted styles into a pleasing, colorful background for the riot of color of the people and the products displayed in the show windows.

Neal St., which winds its way down toward Covent Garden, has a more relaxed and less pressured look with small shops at street level in the two- and three-story buildings built early in the 20th century. Floral St. is a more upscale, fashion-wise street that is situated only two or three streets away from the madness that is Covent Garden.

MELROSE AVE.

LOS ANGELES, CA

Hip! Cool! Trendy! Way Out! Way In!: whatever is the newest, most exciting and most "outre" is sure to be found on Melrose Ave. in Los Angeles. Even before the popularity of "Melrose Place," this area of tired, uninspired architecture—often much the worse for wear and previous lack of care—has attracted the young in search of what is unconventional and non-traditional.

Bright colors, painted facades, names that defy description or explanation, and signs that attempt to explain what is happening where, shocking images, and outlandish style statements are scrambled together for fun and fashionable restaurants are interspersed along with trend setting fashion houses.

Melrose Ave. for fun, for funky and for a fresh and audacious streetscape.

Color, graphics and dimensional signs add to the fun and folly that is fabulous Melrose Ave.

N E W B E R R Y & B O Y L S T O N S T S .

B O S T O N , M A

Gracious old buildings and elegant residences that have gone commercial gently coexist on Newberry and Boylston Streets in the refined Back Bay area of old Boston.

It was in this area, and often on these streets, that the wealthy Bostonians built their palatial homes, churches, and public buildings during the Victorian era and into the first decade of the 20th century. Only a few decades ago this was where only the fashionable and affluent Bostonians would or could shop, but the times they are changing.

Today, designer boutiques and top grade merchants share these streets with more popular price, nationally advertised brands. However, through all the changes and the influx of tourists and the trendy young shoppers, the streetscape still exudes the charm of the bygone era, and the elegant, gracious and often ornately trimmed buildings still stand, recognizable as what they once were. The fun and "for the young" shops pay their respects to the location and somewhat sublimate their image for the overall look and character of the street.

New superimposed over old or new built
next to the established make up the special
look of this Back Bay shopping area.

FELLS POINT

BALTIMORE, MD

Located at the very end of Broadway is the old seaport neighborhood of Fells Point. Old houses from several centuries are clustered together on small, cobblestoned streets which are occasionally interrupted by a small tract of greenery. The old seamen's traditions are still everywhere to be seen as are the nautical references in the architecture, the small business and eateries—and in the daily life of the residents of Fell's Point.

Now that it has been given "tourist" status due to the popularity of "Homicide" on TV, and because of visitors looking for "quaint" and "old" areas to roam, Fells Point is one of the featured stops on the ferry that traverses the Inner Harbor. There has been a rebirth of retail and restaurant business—bars and coffee shops—even theaters and places of entertainment. The citizens of this neighborhood have accommodated to the tastes and peculiarities of the visitors who wander on

the old streets with their gas-lit lamp posts but they have retained the fabric, the weathered and worn texture and the personality of their streetscapes with shingles, faded and worn bricks, marble stoops eroded by age and use, white gone gray with grime, shutters and louvers and shopfronts that have defied the passing years. That is the essence of the Fells Point streetscape.

CHINATOWN

SAN FRANCISCO, CA

Noted for having the largest Chinese community outside of mainland China, Chinatown in downtown San Francisco is an enclave that encompasses 24 blocks of restaurants, souvenir, jewelry , and import stores, museums, hundreds of high rise, walk-up buildings where people live—and

shopping, shopping, shopping. In addition to attracting thousands of tourists each year in search of "local color" and Oriental arts and crafts, it is also home to a multitude of Asians who live, work, shop and eat—all located behind the colorful, dragon festooned archway at Grant and Bush streets. The arch serves as the official entrance to Chinatown.

Half of the fun of being in Chinatown is being tempted and then seduced by the food offerings in the countless restaurants and dim sum shops crowded into the people and merchandise clogged streets. The cacophony of the busy trafficked streets is second only to the visual onslaught of signage in a variety of languages and calligraphy that bombards the visitors. They add the color and spice to the already exotic and exciting venue.

HUNDERTWASSER BUILDINGS

VIENNA, AUSTRIA

Off the beaten tourist path, in a residential area of Vienna, is the Hundertwasser Housing Project and the Hundertwasser Museum. The project is the dream and the vision of the artist/architect/philosopher Hundertwasser.

With the consent of the city planning board of Vienna, Hundertwasser turned an ordinary block (Degelgasse and Lowengasse) into a fantasy of color—of undulating lines and amorphous shapes, textures, tiles and mosaics, glazes and finishes. The facade of the housing project is patterned with bits and pieces of broken tiles and shards of granite and glass. The multi-level houses form a complex of serpentine forms and shapes. The structures seem animated and the design is filled with unexpected nuances and surprises such as trees growing out of windows several stories up. Even the sidewalks are paved with an amalgam of materials and nowhere is there a harsh or clearly defined straight line. The pavement rolls and undulates underfoot.

HUNDERTWASSER MUSEUM

VIENNA, AUSTRIA

The museum, located only a few streets away from the housing project is similar in concept. In keeping with Hundertwasser's theories of living in balance with our environment, trees are incorporated into the facade design since they were removed from street level to make room for the building.

"Man feels sheltered and safe again there where nature and art reunite and man can regain a living part of his own good consciousness towards nature."

"If we do not honor our past, we cannot grow. If we destroy our roots—we cannot grow."

SAN ISIDRO

LIMA, PERU

Think "Lima," think of Latin America, "colorful," "charming," and maybe even "quaint." However, everything is up-to-date in Lima and there are many buildings that reach up to 30 or 40 stories high. San Isidro is an upscale area in Lima with many gracious and expensive high rise condos for the affluent Peruvians and they share the area with sprawling, low slung and garden enclosed homes.

The high rise structures are contemporary and as extraordinary as you might expect to find in an high rent district anywhere in the U.S.–but with a difference. The difference is color. Balconies, balustrades, sweeping curves, patterns of fenestration, handsome and dramatic entrances, porticos and everywhere rich green foliage, trees and flowering plants. This is no small achievement for a city where it seldom rains and plants and flowers must be hand fed and nurtured.

Lima is a city where color finishes the facades of stucco or cement buildings and homes. Even in San Isidro the color element is evident in the streetscape though here it is often tastefully subdued.

KBG CONDOS

GREAT NECK, NY

DESIGN: MOJO STUMER, ROSLYN, NY

PHOTOGRAPHY: TOM LEIGHTON

Precariously located between commercial and industrial neighborhoods, and yet still part of the affluent suburban community of Great Neck, this 55 unit, luxury condominium is part of the streetscape. The other part of the project is a four story aluminum paneled office building with a marble courtyard between it and the condo.

The building configuration was the result of directing views—as much as possible—away from the adjacent buildings by providing the inner courtyard of greenery as the prime focus. The articulation of a balcony for each unit was seen as an amenity as well as a means of expressing the building's use. They also tend to break down the building's scale to more human, intimate and personal units.

ALERT FIREHOUSE

GREAT NECK, NY

DESIGN: MOJO STUMER, ROSLYN, NY

PHOTOGRAPHER: TOM LEIGHTON

The red brick used to face this new firehouse was selected to complement the surrounding domestic architecture in the heart of the village. "Though it stands out from the upscale homes that surround it in this gentrified North Shore town on Long Island, it still becomes an integral part of the streetscape."

"The brick offers visual strength and anchors the structure while enhancing the stainless steel, glass and red panel system that celebrates and also makes reference to the fire truck through its creative use of these exciting materials." The articulated brick details also respect "the human scale of proportion."

The 18,000 sq. ft. building on two levels has been welcomed into the community and has become part of the texture and color of the village because it is "indigenous to its environment."

PORT ORLEANS RESORT

ORLANDO, FL

DESIGN: FUGELBERG KOCH,
WINTER PARK, FL

PHOTOGRAPHY: PHIL ESCHBACH,
ESCHBACH PHOTOGRAPHER,
WINTER PARK, FL

Part of the expanding, theme oriented hotel properties in Disneyworld in Florida is Port Orleans. The hotel/resort, with over 1,000 rooms, was designed by Fugelberg Koch who drew from an architectural vocabulary typical of New Orleans. They used the concept of "a Garden District streetscape" to recreate a strong themed element—"to bring the scale of the large buildings down to a comfortable 'user friendly' level and to manufacture 'street charactered' pedestrian ways for an on-campus movement."

By utilizing a variety of roof lines and color and exterior design elements, the architects were able to reduce large singular buildings into a streetscape of smaller row houses that have the casual charm and yet some of the elegance of the New Orleans neighborhood.

OLD KEY WEST RESORT

ORLANDO, FL

DESIGN: FUGELBERG KOCH,
WINTER PARK, FL

PHOTOGRAPHY: PHIL ESCHBACH,
ESCHBACH PHOTOGRAPHY,
WINTER PARK, FL

What was originally Disney's Vacation
Club is now the Old Key West Resort and
it mirrors a strong traditional Florida theme.
The make-believe neighborhood reflects
the fun, the flash and the fabled "Prohibition
Era" in Key West when it was a point of

entry for illegal liquor. To create the desired streetscape, the architects have designed what appears to be a harborside street consisting of different "houses" for shops, bike rentals, food and beverages and even the sales office facilities.

According to the design firm, "Complete with a lighthouse, the streetscape evokes a setting reminiscent of Downtown Duval Street," in Key West with its color, its architecture and the structural materials.

DIXIE LANDINGS RESORT

ORLANDO, FL

DESIGNER/ARCHITECT:
FUGLEBERG KOCH ARCHITECTS,
WINTER PARK, FL

PHOTOGRAPHER: PHIL ESCHBACH,
ESCHBACH PHOTOGRAPHERS,
WINTER PARK, FL

As illustrated in the previous projects, Fugleberg Koch Architects have created several resorts in Orlando, FL that are all part of Walt Disney World. Each resort is designed to reflect a specific resort theme and "portray a 'streetscape' similar to what one might find if actually in the setting from which the theme was derived."

Dixie Landing Resort, as sister resort to Port Orleans, draws its strong southern design imagery from what could have been a riverboat landing settlement somewhere along the Mississippi a hundred or more

years ago. The themed resort is complete with a cotton gin, boatworks, harbor master and riverboat area.

The streetscape design elements appear in the common area with the assorted period styled facades, pavement, signage, bridge and dockage elements. All the resorts have a common area with the registration, restaurants, retail shops and also the assorted clusters of hotel buildings which are varied in design, in size, and with differing rooflines, materials and facade finishes.

RESTON TOWN CENTER

RESTON, VA

DESIGN: RTKL ARCHITECTS, BALTIMORE, MD

PHOTOGRAPHY: MAXWELL MACKENZIE

The 15 acre, four block "Phase One" of Reston Town Center encompasses two 250,000 sq. ft. office buildings, a 510 room Hyatt Regency Hotel and 150,000 sq. ft. of retail and cinemas—all the while evoking a contemporary "Main Street" character. The prize winning solution uses the mirror image, 11-story Fountain Square buildings to create a "gateway" to the development and as "the beginnings of a recognizable skyline" for the project. "The profile of the towers and the individualized facades of the street level shops echo the picturesqueness of original Reston."

The architects used a variety of building materials, an irregular massing scheme and a full palette of texture and color to give Phase One "a common identity yet a stimulating degree of variation in appearance." With this beginning, RTKL has set "a civic scale and sense of importance" that will affect the future phases of the 85 acre Reston Town Center development.

TLAQUEPAQUE

SEDONA, AZ

"Tlaquepaque is masonry and metal, mission bells and bird song. Tlaquepaque is tiled walkways lined with flowers, historic wrought iron gates and balcony railings, sunbaked courtyards, gracious fountains, splendid archways and cobblestone drives."

Tlaquepaque is also an arts/crafts/dining and entertainment venue surrounded by the fabulous red rock formations of Sedona.

This is not just a streetscape—but an entire village that has been fabricated and then located in this tourist town as a shopping/dining destination. The streetscapes here are complete with two story high buildings with balconies dripping foliage and flowers, a small intimate chapel, a central square just right for fiestas and carnivals, sculpture and so much more. The landscaping—trees,

flowers and shrubs—like the old sycamore trees that were there before the new Tlaquepaque arose, are all part of the grand scheme of this development. Flowering plants and greens are rotated between the grounds and the hothouses "to provide a constantly changing visual— almost sensual—delight."

This exquisite neighborhood is a dream given reality by Abe Miller, a Nevada businessman who was impressed with the architecture and lifestyle of Mexico— and the physical beauty of Sedona. Tlaquepaque is the Indian word for "the best of everything" and here it is the best of two cultures. Arizona Highways, the magazine, printed: "In a setting of superlative natural qualities man has created something of beauty, quaintness and picturesque design that makes it almost impossible to close the eyes and contain the soul."

TRAILDUST TOWN

SCOTTSDALE, AZ

DESIGN: DAN BATES, DESIGN DIRECTOR,
ARGO LAND & CATTLE, TUSCON, AZ

Traildust Town is a charming postcard pretty made-to-order "neighborhood." It is a collection of little houses and reproductions of retail establishments of the late 19th century in Arizona. In addition to the shops and houses there is an Opry House, rough planked walks with timber arcade above and a "saloon" that is now a popular steak house. A lovely gazebo stands in the center of a grassy square that is outlined with trees. This is "Little House on the Prairie" with everything romanticized, squeaky clean and ironed. Whatever is "worn" or "faded" has been artificially produced by an artisan or craftsperson for the effect.

The shopfronts are protected by the projecting wood canopy that also serves as a sun screen and a variety of cornices and roof tops add interest to the streetscape as they stick up above the unifying horizontal frieze.

Directly in front of the Gazebo is the town square with the Saloon and Opry House behind it.

COCOWALK

DESIGN: DEVELOPMENT DESIGN GROUP, BALTIMORE, MD

PHOTOGRAPHY: ARCHITECT & OWNER

Though Coconut Grove is part of Greater Miami, it is a destination unto itself and over three million diners/shoppers make Cocowalk—"a must-see." The 165,000 sq. ft. area is "a cutting edge specialty center combining retail shopping with entertainment, themed night clubs, restaurants and

movies." There is something here for everyone and anytime: from easy strolling in the A.M. to a breakfast/brunch/lunch stop to relaxed shopping in amusing specialty stores—a visit to the movies or a night out in one of the fun night spots.

Cocowalk, designed by Development Design Group, is a three level space filled with open, brick panel courtyards, sweeping staircases, old country arcades, vistas

for viewing and places for sitting. The shops and restaurants are tucked away in one of the two buildings that frame the space or in the circular pavilion, in the center, with its balustrated stairways and balconies and the curved pools.

All of Cocowalk's architecture is outlined in lights and highlighted with ribbons of multi-colored neons. By day, the center is relaxed, casual and Old Floridian, but at

night with lights twinkling and neon flashing—the space exudes the spirit of a carnival or mardi gras.

Because of its distinctive architecture and it unique ambience that combines a local tropical flavor with metropolitan glamor, Cocowalk is often selected as a setting for movies or TV commercials. These add even more theater, entertainment and excitement to the center.

EVERLAND FESTIVAL WORLD

SEOUL, KOREA

DESIGN: DUELL CORP., LOS ANGELES, CA

Part of a giant complex that encompasses 3700 acres is the Festival World, the theme park area that creates a streetscape that encapsulates most of the world.

Festival World's main entrance street, illustrated here, consists of buildings in architectural styles from many lands: from replicas, in scale, of the Taj Mahal and the Victorian Paris Exhibition Pavilion of 1889 to a French Gothic chateau and pre-revolution Russian churches. Assorted retail stores and restaurants fill these exotic buildings as does a 1,000 seat entertainment area for special shows and guest appearances. Also part of the theme park are areas devoted to other amusement "adventures": the American Adventure (rides and roller coasters); Magic Land (for children); European Adventure (gardens and snow slopes for sledding), and Equatorial Adventure (a safari bus tour).

To still be developed at Everlands are Caribbean Bay (indoor/outdoor water park), Safari Zoo World, The Four Seasons Garden, as well as hotels, golf courses, resort complexes and residential areas.

CAMDEN TOWN

LONDON, ENGLAND

PHOTOGRAPHY: MMP/RVC

Camden Town is where the young, anti-fashion "fashionables" go to shop on week-ends. Located at the northern end of London, at the Camden Locks, is Camden Town, a long neighborhood "High Street" of three and four story, nondescript and often brilliantly painted buildings of the early 20th century. What makes it so unique today is the vitality of the retail scene as merchandise seems to gush out of jammed and crammed street level shops, the crush of pushcarts laden with trinkets and trash, the food stalls and stands, and the kiosks and shops that over-whelm the area with wonderful and exotic aromas of ethnic foods. Lording over all are the over life-size, three-dimensional "signs" suspended over the colorful awnings that add even more color to an already riotous street scene. Geared towards the young, the rebellious, the anti-establishment and yet very fashion aware, these "retail sculptures" add humor and enthusiasm to a street bursting with life and excitement.

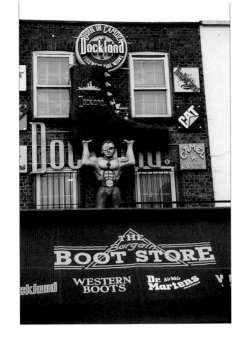

OLD TOWNS

HAMPSTEAD

LONDON, ENGLAND

Though only a very few short miles from Camden Town, Hampstead seems like centuries away in architecture—and eons away when it comes to class and style. Let me quote from a 1922 edition of The Blue Guide to London, "On the N.W. margin of London is a pleasant residential quarter in a 3.5 sq. mile area." This is Hampstead.

Standing in the center of Old Hampstead—the junction of Heath and High Streets is the landmark tube station. According to the Blue Guide this area "deserves a visit for its heath, its views, its literary associations, and its picturesque 18th century houses, and quaintly irregular streets, courts and alleys." Today, much of Hampstead is still charming and quaint though quite up-to-date. The tube station still stands and serves as do many old Georgian homes, the twisting alleys paved in cobblestone and slate, the mews, the crooked lanes that connect main streets and the assortment of chimneys rising above the uneven roof line of the streetscape.

This has become the fashionable place to live for smart and sophisticated Londoners. Though it is only 15 minutes away, by tube, from the entertainment and shopping central London has to offer, this is a self-contained community with shopping, dining and living that combines the best for an upscale lifestyle. Designer and noted brand name outlets are wedged into the wonderful old buildings that line the main streets along with restaurants serving diverse ethnic foods.

Gentle hills, old trees and even older church spires combine with the current retail and dining places to create a unique streetscape for Hampstead.

THE LAB

BRISTOL ST., COSTA MESA, CA

DESIGNER/ARCHITECT: POMPEI A.D., NEW YORK, NY

PHOTOGRAPHER: TOM BONNER

The 38,000 sq. ft. retail/entertainment complex in Orange County is made up of three rehabbed warehouse buildings on Bristol St. in Costa Mesa—just a five minute ride from the upscale South Coast Mall. This "anti-mall" shopping center consists of about two dozen retail outlets, two restaurants, a public gathering space and a theater playhouse. The center caters to a very specific crowd: mainly 18-30–Generation Xers and the space is anchored by Urban Outfitters which, like The Lab, was designed by Pompei, A.D. of New York. The unconventional center is most unique.

The original warehouse buildings were gutted, walls were sand blasted, sheets of rusted corrugated and plate metal revealed or added along with scraps of used lumber, old doors, window frames, antique signs, twisted and tortured metal pipes and signage—all finished in soft, sun-bleached colors. Together they create the deconstructionist look that can be called "recycled"—if a style name must be applied. One of the focal elements in The Lab is the "fountain" which was formed from old doors, slabs of concrete and barrels left over from the original structures.

In addition to Urban Outfitters, The Lab is home to Tower Records, Crew Salon, Spanish Fly and other "outrageous" Generation X-oriented stores. The Lab also features an on-site vegetable and herb garden for the ecology conscious as well as live musical performances, poetry readings and art galleries for the young culturals.

The Lab showcases these "alternative retailers" in the anti-mall setting for an audience that cares for more than what is "hot" and what is "cool." It is a thinking person's shopping experience where one can take time out to listen to the music, feel the poetry, relax before the recycled fountain and just smell the roses—or the herbs.

SOUTH END BREWERY/COTTON ST. DINER

SOUTH END, CHARLOTTE, NC.

DESIGN: SHOOK DESIGN GROUP, CHARLOTTE, NC

PHOTOGRAPHER: TIM BUCHMAN

The redevelopment of the long neglected South End area of Charlotte is exemplified by the two restaurants shown here. Shook Design Group, the architectural/design firm is involved in the refurbishing and the revitalizing of this old area with its aging factory buildings. In the plans for Camden Square, as the rehabbed area will be called, is a multi-purpose complex consisting of entertainment, retail, restaurants, residences and office space. There will be some new buildings but the older ones will be rehabbed, cleaned up, brick facades linked by dramatic arches, landscaping, courtyards and promenades.

Kevin Kelley, co-founder of Shook Design Group and president of South End Development Corp., said, "The trend in Charlotte is what's happening across the U.S. Everyone is tired of suburbia: it may even be a backlash to all the technology that modern day has provided us. When urban areas are revitalized, there's a sense of culture, pride and history. It gets into people's psyche more than anything. People like going into an old building to eat."

South End Brewery is located in Atherton Mill which is situated at the far south end of this to-be-revitalized area. The mill is a six building complex which in addition to the brewery, houses a gallery and some retail stores. The architects converted the almost dilapidated two story warehouse into a 14,000 sq. ft. restaurant. The front was "extensively reworked in order to achieve the aesthetic design and maintain the structural integrity of the space." The existing stucco finish was revealed when metal plates were removed from the facade and larger windows were installed on the main restaurant level. Throughout, the architects worked within the zoning restrictions. The brew tank in the patio carries signage which can be seen from two sides and the name also appears on the front entrance.

The Cotton St. Diner was transformed from a nondescript, traditional style restaurant into this flavorsome, upscale Diner that is suited to the ambiance of the surrounding neighborhood and the streetscape. The design concept is based on a 1920s service station becoming a diner with counter service in the 1930s. The diner continues to be enlarged and "added on" to until the 1960s. The architects took advantage of the height of the new structure with vertical wedge elements that are carried through on the interior. A wide expanse of fenestration is introduced as well as the relocation of the main entry.

UNION ST. & FENIMORE ST.

SAN FRANCISCO, CA

They are not all gone, nor are they forgotten. The thousands of Victorian houses built of wood then adorned with myriad moldings, trimmed with turrets and tiles, accented with arches and other architectural furbelows and then finally painted in a rainbow of colors, are still there. Not as many—not as colorful and maybe not as "pure" and virginal as they were a century ago—but still prized and treasured. In the book "Painted Ladies" by M. Baer, E. Pomada and M. Larsen, it says, "The Painted Ladies of San Francisco are exquisite examples of how an American tradition worth saving can be revitalized and made meaningful to a new generation."

Some of these Painted Ladies still proudly present themselves as part of the streetscape while others have been rehabbed, retouched, or even renovated to serve the needs of the young, outgoing, fun-loving society of San Francisco. Bars, coffee shops, craft and clothing stores mix it up with banks, real estate and law offices on Union and Fenimore Sts. as well as those around them, and uniquely pay tribute to a time past, by taking up residence in these grand old and colorful remnants that are pure San Francisco.

OAK PARK, IL

Just minutes away from Chicago is Oak Park where early in the 20th century Frank Lloyd Wright, the great American architect, lived, designed and created the streetscapes that still exist as a tribute to his Prairie Style of Architecture.

As a compliment to the architect as well as the honesty and integrity of his work, many Wright-designed homes still stand as do some of the religious and secular buildings he designed in Oak Park.

A walk down several tree shaded streets is a stroll down pages of American Architecture from 1893 to 1912 and an opportunity to see unchanged, unmodified and untampered with the Master's work.

His concepts changed the face and form of American homes and tastes in decoration.

His studio/home has also been renovated and refurbished with many original Wright furniture and decorative pieces.

As a streetscape, it is small town America in the first part of the 20th century—as it was and still is.

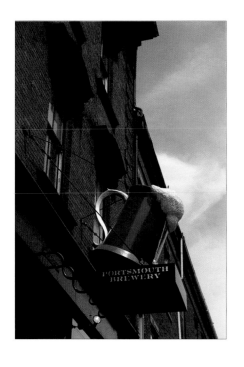

PORTSMOUTH, NH

A walk through the charming old streets of the port city of Portsmouth is like a stroll through the early 19th century. The town has been rediscovering its heritage and is now flaunting its traditions and history by polishing up its visual image and refreshing its approach to retailing.

The buildings are not all that old or that interesting. Some do date back 200 years while others are only 100 or so years old. Many are just a conglomeration of wood and brick houses—residential and commercial—two or three stories high that were built after the turn into the 20th century. But everything is up-to-date by looking old and all eyes are on the signs of Portsmouth.

Everywhere—extending out at right angles from buildings or attached to them are the wonderfully clever, wood carved, colored, gilt enhanced dimensional signs that illustrate what is sold where, and where what services can be obtained. Canvas awnings, planters filled with flowers and shrubs, trees growing out of the narrow sidewalks, gas type lamp posts, benches for the weary, side walk cafes and small coffee shops, colorful umbrellas and always the signs on the multi-textured buildings add to a definite streetscape look for old/new downtown Portsmouth.

CREEK ST.

KETCHIKAN, AK

Remnant of a time gone by but now revived and rehabbed to a fun and funky tourist attraction in Ketchikan, is Creek St. Back at the turn of the last century and the start of the 20th century, these colorful and often askew shacks on stilts that are lined up along the timber walkway, were filled with bars, brothels and the "bad" women who lived here. Today they house craft shops, galleries, souvenir stands, coffee shops and fast food establishments, and even—on dry land—some B & B houses.

The developers have attempted to keep and actually accentuate the "rough and ready" mining town ambiance of that long ago time because that is what the tourists—coming off the cruise ships that pull in almost daily—aspect. It is what they expect the Klondike to have looked like during the Gold Rush days.

FANEUIL
HALL
MARKETPLACE

BOSTON, MA

This festival Marketplace which was renovated, rehabbed and revitalized 20 years
ago is a classic and much duplicated prototype of urban renewal. Located between
the towering skyscrapers of Boston's
Financial Center and the North End where
Paul Revere's home and the Old North
Church still serve as beacons for tourists in
this old Italian neighborhood, Faneuil Hall
and the Quincy Market are filled with
retail shops, colorful kiosks, restaurants
and outdoor entertainment.

The market buildings that form a three
sided frame around the historic Faneuil Hall
date back to 1826 and the red brick structures still serve as a retail setting for clothing and souvenir shops. In addition to the
flower market, the live entertainment and
the colorful blitz of banners, flags and
balloons, The Haymarket, on weekends,
provides a cornucopia of foods, produce
and exotic delicacies for the locals of the
North End and the tourists that fill the
Marketplace.

BARCELONA, SPAIN

To a visitor, it would appear that time has stopped ticking in Barcelona and nothing is new—nothing has changed—and all is as it was a century ago. But that opinion would be based solely on the streetscapes of this wonderful city in northern Spain where famous buildings, unaffected by civil war or world strife, still stand to be admired and be used by the citizens and their guests.

This is the city of Gaudi—of Art Nouveau—of whip-lash lines, of swirling, sweeping and surprising structures and caprices that defy the eye and to whom straight lines are an anathema. Here are buildings accented with color, textured with sculptured reliefs, rounded edges on corner buildings to complement the rounded line of the side-walk, balconies enriched with wrought iron fantasies accentuated by stained glass panels and windows. Gaudi's buildings are topped with chimneys that are works of art finished in tiles, mosaics, pieces of glass, and they add a unique quality to the skylines of many main thoroughfares.

Beaux Arts beauties of French influence cohabit with the curvacous domestic and commercial structures of the Gaudi tradition—all in a streetscape textured with trees, shrubs, and flower plants.

More of the wonderful curves and
sweeping arcs that gave the late 19th
century architecture of Barcelona its
distinctive look.

BELLAVISTA

SANTIAGO, CHILE

Not only tourists, but the Chileans themselves, flock to this old, quasi-historic Bellavista area across the river to enjoy "La Vie Boheme." This old section of decrepit and nondescript houses has leased a new life as an entertainment and crafts center in Santiago.

Old buildings have been refreshed and revitalized with new stucco finishes, bright and audacious colors that are teamed up

to clash and jump off the facades and awnings and planters. Discos, restaurants, odd clothing shops, jewelry and craft stores and galleries co-mingle amid the often shocking and jarring colors. Some of the older side streets maintain their faded dignity though still in harmony with the excitement around them. On a sunny Sunday afternoon, all of Belavista is on display with artisans and salespeople presenting their wares on the cracked sidewalks—adding more color and texture to the streetscape.

LA BOCA

BUENOS AIRES, ARGENTINA

La Boca is the old port section of Buenos Aires where many Italian families settled when they migrated from Genoa more than a century ago. With them they brought their humor, their sense of color and their pleasure in being alive.

Though there are local bars and restaurants, small shops and many galleries, what really draws visitors to this area to shop and spend time is the local COLOR. The local COLOR is wild, strong, brash and uninhibited in how and where it is applied—when and why it is used. The colors are used for the excitement of seeing the surrounding—often tired and decrepit old houses, shanties and shacks turned into "Art" by the paintbrush wielding natives.

The residents of La Boca revel in their color filled streetscapes and they add additional blobs of color with clotheslines laden with tints, hues and shades. Artists roam freely or sit quietly trying to capture on canvas the feeling of this neighborhood which they then sell to the busloads of tourists who come to see where the Tango was born.

GRAFTON ST.

DUBLIN, IRELAND

Bounded by the lovely old Georgian buildings of Trinity College on the north and St. Stephen's Green and the Victorian-style glass and iron "greenhouse" mall on the south, Grafton St. is only four streets long but it is Fashion all of the way. Grafton St. is THE shopping street of Dublin along with the neighboring Dawson St. and the small, crooked, cobblestoned lanes that lead off Grafton St.

The city fathers and landmark preservationists have done a remarkable job in maintaining the late Victorian architecture and texture of this streetscape. From 15 ft. off the slate and brick paved pedestrian thoroughfare—with the exception of fresh coats of paint and the flowering window boxes—nothing seems to have changed in the last 100 years. Below that, the shopfronts have been redesigned to respect the architecture above and though often contemporary, they rarely ever clash or denigrate the look of this "period" street. Display windows are lightly trimmed with the newest and trendiest fashions. There are

book and record shops, the famous old Bewley's Oriental Tea House, dozens and dozens of clocks and the fast food shops. Even McDonald's and Burger King have been toned down to maintain the dignity and the look of the street.

Adding some local color are the abundant open air flower stands, the street musicians, the made-up mimes, and the old fashioned gas lamps—now converted to electricity—that at night add halos of warm light to the brick laid pavement below. Some of the major stores such as Arnotts, Marks & Spencer and Brown Thomas take refuge behind facades composed of several old buildings unified by paint and then illuminated by up-lights at night. The interiors have been gutted and completely renovated to accommodate the needs and pleasures of the new shoppers.

In keeping with the look, the feel and the texture of Dublin, Grafton St. with all its Victorian heritage is truly Old Town at its best for the throngs of shoppers who fill the streets today.

Grafton Street, Dublin, Irerland
Right: San Francisco, California

WELLS FARGO BANK

BIG BUSINESS

MARKET STREET

SAN FRANCISCO, CA

Market St. is the "stock market" street in downtown San Francisco. It is where big business is housed in bigger and bigger buildings built in between the classic reminders of the early 20th century.

Almost as if in deference to the large Asian population in San Francisco and the invest-ment capital from across the Pacific Ocean, many of the newer structures sport curves and rounded corners. Not only are the arcs part of Feng Shui (The Art of Placement) but they complement the older, classically inspired buildings snuggled in between the strong, vertical towers. At street level the doorways and portals speak of different architectural styles of this century—of different times and traditions.

PORTLAND, OR

The streetscape of Portland's downtown area does not have the sky reaching towers of New York or even Dallas, but it is filled with high rise commercial buildings of the early 20th century. They speak of a time when downtown Portland was a busy, bustling shopping area of noted department stores and specialty shops. These handsome and highly ornamented glazed terra cotta facades were the homes of the department stores, the banking facilities and commercial offices.

Today, the decorative old-timers share the downtown with not so sky scraping commercial towers that are not pylons but vertical structures accented with dramatic angles, cuts and slashes and accented with color. Together they stand witness to the revival of downtown Portland as a commercial, cultural and retail center that still has a relaxed and casual charm about it

BOSTON, MA

Big business and big buildings go together in Boston in the area near the waterfront and the historic area of Faneuil Hall. Giant corporations have built gigantic structures to house their worldwide, commercial endeavors. One bank building attempts to outreach and outdesign the next bank building—which is located right next to it. An occasional park or accent of greenery relieves the stone, steel and glass textures of the streetscapes of commercial Boston.

The shimmer and shine of the reflective glass and metal surfaces are complemented by accents of color, flashes of gilt, and even sculptural entrances into these super structures off the narrow, crowded streets.

WORLD TRADE CENTER/BATTERY PARK

NEW YORK, NY

At the tip of the island of Manhattan is the financial center of New York and much of the world. How the island still stands under the weight of the skyscrapers, towers, commercial structures, even malls, museums and other civic and cultural centers is a mystery.

The marble, granite and glass materials, the slick and smooth textures broken only by the reflective glass and the dramatic shadows of the forms and shapes interacting with the occasional welcome sweep of arches, arcs and curves, create a unique streetscape for this busy part of New York.

Tucked in amid the high risers are buildings from the 1910s and the roaring, soaring 1920s when everything boomed and everybody built bigger and more decorative buildings. They are symbols of a time when there were no boundaries on how tall to build. Like many other cities, it is the mix of old and new and of the decorated and the decorous that distinguishes the big city, big business

HAAS HAUS

VIENNA, AUSTRIA

DESIGN: HANS HOLLEIN, VIENNA, AUSTRIA

PHOTOGRAPHY: MMP/RVC

According to the designer/architect of the Haas Haus project in central Vienna, Hans Hollein, "The architectural articulation of the building both internal and external is a volumetric issue." The curved stone skin partially peels off from a structural glass facade. Both these elements float above a double story colonnade which is derived in scale from the surrounding, much older buildings. A rather calm, slightly warped stone facade faces towards Goldschmidtgasse. Between these two facades cylindrical forms intersect with cubes and push forward—above the entrance—into the space between Stock im Eisen and St. Stephan's Plaza. Stone provides the continuity for "contextual architectural reasons as well as aesthetic requirements." Light colored stones were selected: Spluga Verde for its "neutral serenity" and accents of Verde Fontein for the gradation and matching of color.

Haas Haus is a multi-purpose building which combines shopping with office spaces above. It is located across from the venerable St. Stephan's Church whose ornate carved sprockets and spires are mirrored in the reflective areas of the Haas Haus facade As is the upscale shopping area that surrounds this unique building.

CANAL CITY HAKATA

FUKUOKA, JAPAN

ARCHITECTS: THE JERDE PARTNERSHIP INTERNATIONAL, LOS ANGELES, CA

DESIGN: SELBERT PERKINS DESIGN (FORMERLY CLIFFORD SELBERT DESIGN COLLAB.), CAMBRIDGE, MA

CONSULTANTS: LANDSCAPE ARCHITECTURE: EDAW, IRVINE, CA

LIGHTING: JOE KAPLAN ARCHITECTURAL LIGHTING, UNIVERSAL CITY, CA

PHOTOGRAPHER: H. KAWANO

The two million sq. ft. complex built in Hakata in Fukuoka, Japan is composed of an office building, two hotels, retail area and an entertainment district. "The objective of giving an identity and theme to the vast complex resulted in giving the city a universal soul—on a human scale it communicates to Hakata residents, international business, industry and tourists." The architects, the Jerde Partnership International of Los Angeles, joined creative forces with Selbert Perkins Design to create this excit-

ing, multi-media, multi-use and multi-faceted cityscape. To visually differentiate the five distinct areas of the complex, the designers added 50 ft. tall, three dimensional towers of stainless steel with etched bases which serve as focal points as well as directionals within Canal City. The towers carry distinctive logos/sculptures and names: Sun Plaza, Star Court, Moon Walk, Earth Walk and Sea Court.

The canal in Canal City is the most important connecting link in the design of the complex. It arcs through the center and "creates not only dynamic scenery but facilitates the building identification and circulation." Like rivers and streams shape the Grand Canyon, the architecture around the central canal is striated—like layers in a canyon. "Textures move from ground level dark then lighter stone, to higher level mirrored surfaces that reflect the sky."

Architecture, landscape design, waterways, lighting and environmental graphics and signage all combine to support the concept "of the universe and the passage of time."

CITRALAND CENTRE GROGOL

JAKARTA, INDONESIA

DESIGN: DEVELOPMENT GROUP, BALTIMORE, MD

The international retail/entertainment/hotel complex is a 93,000 sq. meter, multi-use structure. The nine story high retail center is organized around a dramatic atrium space that has an internal ramp walkway system. In addition to the 310 room hotel, there is also a six story parking building with easy access to the shopping floors.

The dynamic, symmetrical design of Citraland—especially the hotel with its sweeping central facade and the twin towers that rise up on either side—makes a striking addition to the looming skyscrapers that fill the skyline of Jakarta proper.

A K M E R K E Z

I S T A N B U L , T U R K E Y

DESIGN: DEVELOPMENT DESIGN GROUP, BALTIMORE, MD

The rising, blue tinted glass cylinders make a striking statement for the 44,000 sq. meter, four level specialty center/mixed use building in Istanbul. Located in an affluent neighborhood of Istanbul, Akmerkez features department store anchors, extensive fashion retail, entertainment, restaurants, food courts and a cinemaplex at the base of the high rise towers. The upper stories accommodate offices and commercial enterprises as well as an upscale residential development.

The street level shops and restaurants are unified by the architectural design, the colors, and the materials used. The landscaping softens and humanizes the strong contemporary lines of the total project.

EPO

KOTESASHI, JAPAN

DESIGN: KAPLAN, MCLAUGHLIN DIAZ
ARCHITECTS, SAN FRANCISCO, CA

Designed as a prototype for future EPO centers, this 3500 sq. meter specialty retail center in Kotesashi, Japan, has been strategically located diagonally across from a major department store.

Adding emphasis and a focal point to the surrounding streetscape is the skylit public atrium which serves as a community meeting place. Curving forms, colored accents, diagonal striping, and colorful banners combine to create a distinctive look for the center that was designed with flexible outdoor and indoor spaces to accommodate different types of theater and entertainment.

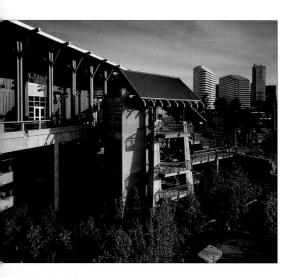

REI

SEATTLE, WA

DESIGN: MITHUN PARTNERS, SEATTLE, WA

According to the architects/designers of the 80,000 sq. ft. REI store, "The flagship store announces the change in Seattle's city street grid by placing the world's tallest, free standing, indoor climbing wall—a new icon at REI— at the corner of the site, providing a new gateway to downtown"—and thus affecting the streetscape of the surrounding area.

The sprawling, multi-level structure is constructed of native stone, timber, steel and glass and "the retail space design and materials reflect a casual, natural atmosphere consistent with REI's outdoor heritage and environment commitment."

An outstanding feature of the total design is the aforementioned climbing wall that is encased in a glass and steel tower. The man-made 65 ft. "mountain" is always on view: it has been programmed with lighting that changes and simulates the path of the sun. From the top of the pinnacle one can view Puget Sound and the Olympic Mountains.

The landscaping surrounding the structure contains a 470 ft. outdoor bike testing track in the courtyard, a still pond and a waterfall amid the 21,000 sq. ft. of native Northwest trees, plants and shrubs.

QUALITY
KING

HAUPPAGAUGE, NY

DESIGN: MOJO STUMER, ROSLYN, NY

PHOTOGRAPHY: FRANK ZIMMERMAN

Set against a background of a corporate park in the town of Islip on Long Island, "This architectural statement of warehouse and office attempts to redefine this building type by inherently expressing the nature of its use."

The 15,000 sq. ft. executive office building flows in a rhythm of forms in a variety of materials while the stark, monolithic 165,000 sq. ft. warehouse is a concrete masonry unit and it is "anchored to the earth." The office building, in contrast, expresses itself in a harmony of glass block, aluminum panels, and a curtain wall "undulating with the activity of life."

The many changes in form and material creates a streetscape of varied movements and impressions that all come together to establish "basic polarity" inherent in this type of architectural use.

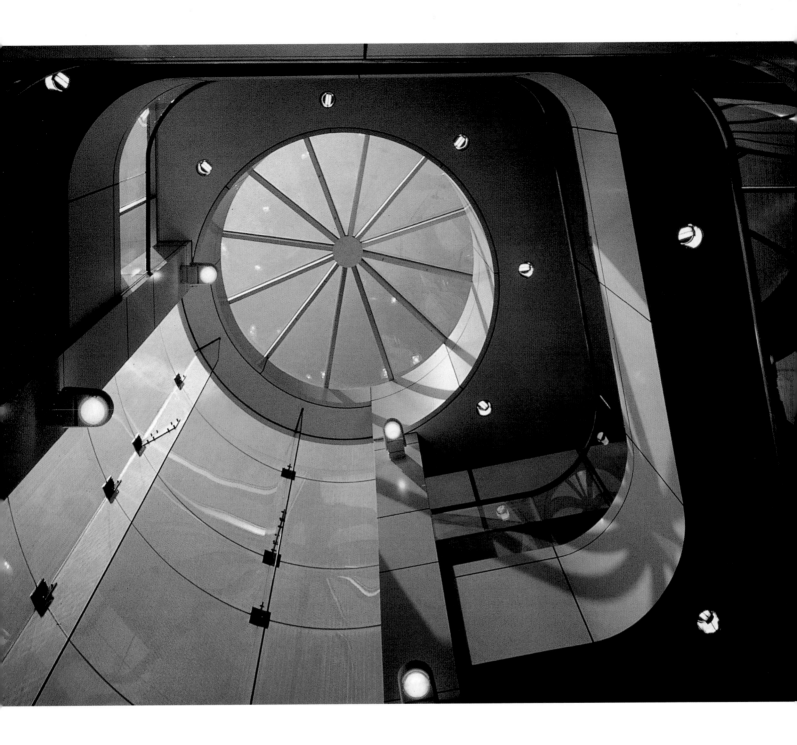

CHINA TRUST BANK

QUEENS, NY

DESIGN: GREENFIELD, SAWICKI, TARELLA ARCHITECTS, NEW YORK, NY

Flushing, Queens is an area that is mainly filled with restaurants, greenmarkets, super- markets and small retailers all catering to a largely Asian clientele—who also happen to live and work there. The China Trust Bank built its new building on Main St.: a street already overflowing with Chinese calligra- phy, signage and traditions. The architec-

tural firm of Greenfield, Sawicki Tarella of New York combined sleek, contemporary architectural concepts with Feng Shui, the Chinese Art of Placement of buildings, doors, furniture, etc. Good Feng Shui allows the cosmic energy—the Chi—to "flow freely through a building, creating a better environment for employees and customers."

The rounded corner entrance encourages people to enter the bank from the two streets and also permits the Chi to move freely around the building without obstructive sharp corners or edges. Though the design was inspired by the China Trust Bank in Taiwan, the American architects used materials such as metal and glass for their affect on the street.

The bank's design won top honors in the category "New Construction–Office Building" and it was cited for continuing the tradition of building "attractive structures that not only advance a community's spiritual and moral character but contribute to the environment (the streetscape) as well."

INNER HARBOR

BALTIMORE, MD

The Harborside of Baltimore is more than picturesque: it is an exciting mixture of hotels, retail malls, entertainment, commercials and cultural buildings all combined with the history of the city.

Structures with highly reflective facades mirror the sky and the water surrounding the buildings and trees add accents of greenery. New hotel and commercial buildings rub shoulders with buildings built in the 1920s and 1930s and even some old brick buildings from the previous cen-

tury. The historic schooners and frigates that line up along the festive pier add to the old/new look of this area while museums and aquariums of startling contemporary design are juxtaposed over this exciting flag, banner and pennant bedecked entertainment collage.

NIGHTSCAPES

The sun goes down. The scene changes. Buildings blur and blend with the night sky. Forms melt away and foreground and background become a black-on-black canvas unrelieved by texture. Landscaping, trees, shrubs and plants vanish into the vast void of night.

A light goes on and the black canvas comes alive. Lights appear all over the canvas—singly, in clusters or in bursts. There are strings of lights blinking and twinkling that outline a roof-line, a cornice, window frames, a doorway. Bands of colored lights wash over the all but invisible structures defining forms, outlining shapes and creating patterns in myriad colors. Ribbons of neon, in a rainbow palette, race around buildings and illuminate and illustrate signs. Uplights, downlights, batteries of lights: incandescent, fluorescent and halides—all together create a streetscape that is a different place with a different face. Facades glow, windows gleam, signs sparkle and the world is electric, vibrant and alive.

On the following pages are visions of various nightscpaes; fashion streets, restaurant rows, downtown and uptowns, entertainment venues, malls and centers, department stores and specialty stores. Singly or as clusters the illuminated buildings becomes focal points in the streetscape and give a new sizzling character to a street or neighborhood.

TIMES SQUARE & BROADWAY

NEW YORK, NY

Starting at 42nd St. and with the arrival of the Disney presence that magically is transforming the formerly run-dow and tawdry street, Broadway and Times Square are once again glittering, glitzy and all aglow with the kinetic pageant of lights. The new restaurants and fast food places on 42nd St. and on Broadway, and the renovated theaters add new spectacle to the already famous panorama of ever-changing billboards of half nude/half clad models and noted fashion names.

The new "big" light show takes place at Virgin Records and the All Star Cafe that neighbor each other on the scandalous street between W. 45 and 46th St.s. Together they are the light focus of night-time Broadway with the swipes of bright red giving way to signage and illuminated illustrations.

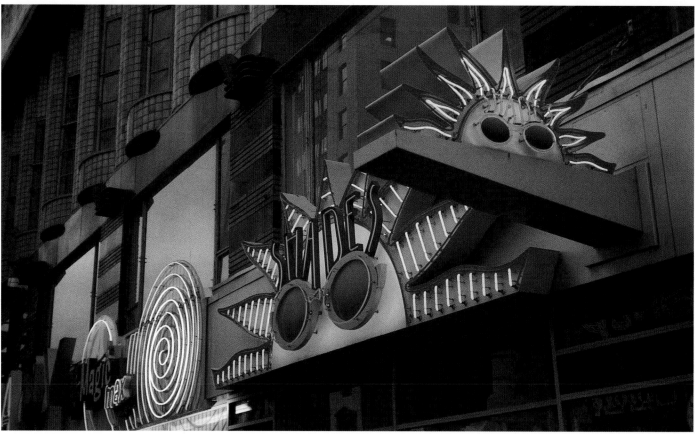

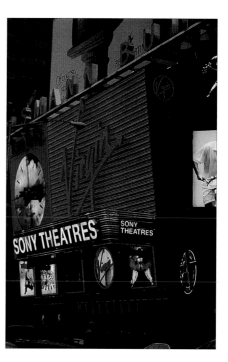

N Y / N Y

LAS VEGAS, NV

For "oh"ing and "ah"ing in the sunlit hours there is nothing—yet quite like the spectacle of the N.Y. City skyline reproduced—in bits and pieces—in scale on Las Vegas Blvd.. At night, the designers tried to capture the essence of NYC's night life and the glow of Metropolis with the signage, facade lighting, window outlining, marquees and canopies.

The spectacle of kinetic patterns created by neon ribbons synchronized by computer makes the underside of the entrance marquee one of Vegas's most sensational sights. The full view of NY/NY, provided by the hotel/resort, shows the excitement generated by the hotel's presence on the Blvd.

LAS VEGAS BLVD.

LAS VEGAS, NV

What would Las Vegas be—at night—without its signs? During the daylight hours, one can travel around the world by walking in a straight line down Las Vegas Blvd., but at night the street becomes a sparkling fantasy of millions of twinkling and flickering bulbs, miles and miles of multi-colored neon streamers and sequins, splash and tinsel. It is all make believe! It is all illusion! It is all sparkle and shine! What is tawdry, shoddy,

schlocky and almost a-shamble is lost in the darkness of night and what the visitor sees is what the designer, the architect, the lighting specialist wants them to see.

Buildings are outlined in ribbons of light, facades are lit up, signs splutter and spurt forth streams of light and the miracle of all this lighting magic is that it happens every night—and all over the city. Here we stroll down the Boulevard and see the hotels illuminated in all their electric splendor.

FREEMONT ST.

LAS VEGAS, NV

DESIGN OF THE ARCHWAY: THE JERDE
PARTNERSHIP, VENICE, CA

The Freemont St. Experience is a dazzling
out-in-the-open, free-for-all, show of lights
that has helped to restore downtown Las
Vegas and the "other" hotel/gaming area
away from the Blvd.

The $70 million "Experience" covers 1400
lineal feet of Freemont St. The space frame
arch is 90 ft. high and spans across 125 ft.

During the day it serves as a 50% sun screen for pedestrians but at night, when the light and sound show goes on, more than two million incandescent bulbs of rainbow colors start to dance, swirl, flash and, like in Busby Berkeley routines of the 1930 musicals, create kaleidoscopic patterns on the towering vaulted construction.

According to the fabricating and installing company, Young Electric Sign Co. of Las Vegas, with the eight shades of dimming there are more than 65,000 color combinations possible. The high intensity strobe lights, robotic mirrors and variable color lighting fixtures add even more excitement to the "sky show."

When the sound and light show goes on, the lights all around are turned off. Before and after the show the individual hotels, casinos and restaurants on either side of the arch on Freemont St. come alive with new signage and facade lighting extavaganzas that rival the high powered presentation one gets strolling along the Las Vegas Blvd.

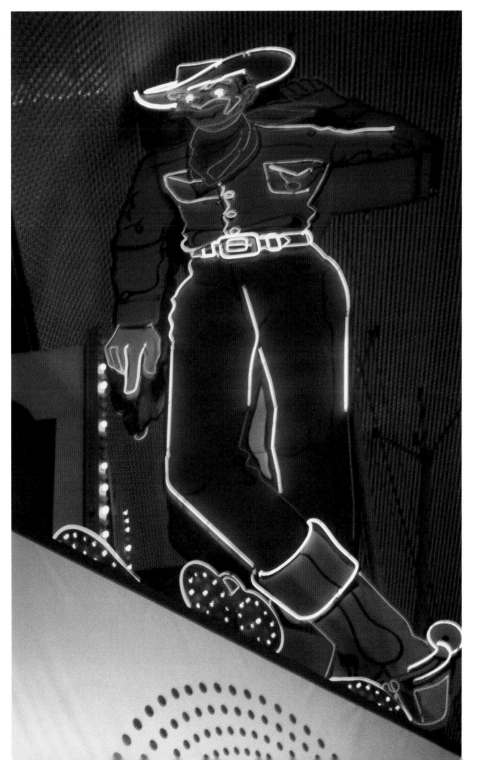

157

Millions of lights flash, flicker and fill the
night-time sky over Fremont St. literally
lighting up the street.

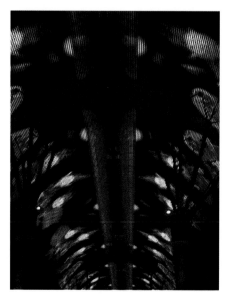

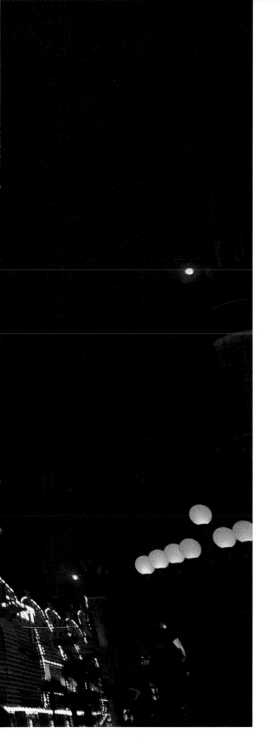

COCOWALK

COCONOT GROVE, FL

DESIGN: DEVELOPMENT DESIGN GROUP, BALTIMORE, MD

PHOTOGRAPHY: ARCHITECT & OWNER

This project, previously shown as it appears during the daylight hours in Coconut Grove (see Neighborhoods), takes on an entirely new persona after sunset. The relaxed, easy-going, Florida lifestyle disappears as the excitement and glitter of neon and incandescents take over the scene. Buildings are outlined, arches are accentuated, fountains illuminated and facades are bathed in hot pastel colored lights.

Over it all is a hot glow that promises and delivers "a hot time in the old town tonight." It is carnival time, Mardi Gras and Broadway and Las Vegas all tossed into one and the result is an eruption of thrilling color.

IRVINE SPECTRUM

IRVINE, CA

DESIGN: RTKL, LOS ANGELES, CA

VP IN CHARGE: PAUL F. JACOB

PROJECT MANAGER: DAVE SCHMITZ

AVP IN CHARGE OF ENVIRONMENTAL GRAPHICS: KATIE J. SPRAGÚE

ENVIRONMENTAL GRAPHICS PROJECT DESIGNER: KEVIN D. HORN

The 270,000 sq. ft. Entertainment Center at Irvine Spectrum is situated in a choice location where two major freeways intersect. The work of the architectural design firm RTKL of Los Angeles, the center draws its visitors and shoppers from the surrounding metropolitan area. The design inspiration is from Southern California's predominantly Spanish Mediterranean architecture. While still maintaining a Mediterranean influence, the RTKL design team introduced some Moroccan overtones in design elements which "speak to simpler issues of mass, light, shadow and color." It is precisely this bolder and stronger statement that helps to balance the intimate human scale environment of the entertainment/retail/restaurant area with the adjacent 124,000 sq. ft. Edwards Cinema.

Public spaces are kept large and open at the cinema end of the project but they gently transition into more intimate, narrow and traditional medina-like passageways one envisions in a Moroccan village. To further humanize the project, the environmental graphics designers on the design team have developed a "softer way finding system" to help visitors navigate the area. "Subdued patterns and clustered elements are used to outline gathering areas and draw people to the heart of the project." The open air plaza, the recurring dome elements, and the centrally situated gazebo are complemented by the bright, imaginative environmental graphics.

The total center consists of seven separate buildings that house retail and restaurant establishments plus the large Edwards Cinema. A 400-seat Oasis Court is located in the open central plaza and is the hub of the eating/shopping experience. Brilliant mosaic, fountains splashing, colorfully bright tent-topped kiosks—the narrow, winding walkways all reinforce the Moroccan theme. At night, when the magical lights come on and take over—the Arabian Night fantasy continues.

CANAL CITY

HAKATA AT NIGHT

DESIGN: JERDE PARTNERSHIP, VENICE, CA

GRAPHICS/SIGNAGE: SELBERT PERKINS DESIGN: CAMBRIDGE, MA

PHOTOGRAPHY: H. KAWANO

What a difference the time of day can make. Refer back to Canal City in the Big Business entry to remind yourself what this multi-use, big business complex looked like in sunshine and now see how the fabulous colored lights and fantastic signage has taken over and transformed the big and bombastic exterior into more intimate, bright and amusing areas by means of highlighting and illuminated signage and graphics on the buildings and the individual streetscape signage scaled to the people on the street.

UNIVERSAL CITY WALK

DESIGN: JERDE PARTNERSHIP, VENICE, CA

The Universal City Walk (see Main St.) also designed by The Jerde Partnership takes on a fiery glow of reds, pinks, oranges and gold when the neon and incandescent not only light up the streets but the sky as well.

The photo of the area, by Stephen Simpson, shows a torrid and scintillating Main St. as a nightscape.

MULTIPLEX
CINEMAS

AMC, ONTARIO
MILLS, ONTARIO, CA

DESIGN: GLYNN BROWN DESIGN,
KANSAS CITY, MO

PHOTOGRAPHY: PHOTO DESIGN,
KANSAS CITY, MO
CINESCAPE, CINEMA ODEON CORP.,
HOUSTON, TX

DESIGN: KIKU OBATA AND COMPANY,
ST. LOUIS, MO

PHOTOGRAPHY: GARY QUESADA

CINESCAPE
CINEMA ODEON CORP.
HOUSTON, TX

DESIGN: KIKU OBATA & CO.
ST. LOUIS, MO

PHOTOGRAPHY: GARY QUESADA

Making a new and tremendous impact on
nightscapes in cities, towns, and along side
malls and centers are the imposing, colorful
and action filled facades and marquees of
the multiplex cinemas. Some are part of
giant entertainment complexes while others
are the destination points of the entertainment seekers.

In addition to staking its claim on the
streetscape and getting the attention it
seeks, the Cinema must also impart infor-
mation; what is playing where and when.
During the daylight hours these multiplex
constructions can rely on colorful materials
and interesting textures to make their
impact on the streetscape, but at night it
takes lights—lots and lots of lights—and all
kinds and colors of light to tell the story.

Whether alone as Kiku Obata's Cinescape
is or as part of the entertainment complex as
GB Design's AMC Theater is, it takes light
to define the building and sell the promise of
entertainment and satisfaction inside.

A

A: AMC The Grand, Dallas, TX.
B: AMC, Huebner Oaks, San Antonio, TX.
C: AMC Indian River, Vero Beach, FL.
Designed by GB Design Inc. and Gould
Evans Goodman, Inc.
Photography: S.J. Swalwell/Architectural
Fotographics (A)/FOTO GRAPHICS
(B/C)

D: Fulton's Crab House, Lake Buena Vista
Designed by Marve Cooper Design,
Chicago, Il.

Three more AMC Cinemaplexes designed by GB Design, Kansas City and Gould Evans Goodman Inc. The Grand 24 in Dallas was, when it was opened, the largest theater complex in the U.S. The giant, sprawling complex glows at night with the combination of up lights and neon ribbons that accentuate the foward sweep in the facade design. As requested by the AMC Corp., the exterior is "exceptionally exciting and a visual experience that builds antici-pation for the patrons" for the entertain-ment that awaits them inside.

At Huebner Oaks in San Antonio, the building organizes itself around a pedestri-an plaza that serves as a focal point and enhances the theater entrance. The free forming canopy, at night, is illuminated to appear a fiery red while during the daylight hours the building reflects a southwest scheme and presents a festive attitude. The AMC theater at Indian River is an impor-tant part of the mall development in Vero Beach. The unique and bold color scheme reflects the southeast region and "achieves an identity that projects cinematic enter-tainments "—especially when it glows at night.

Not a movie house by a fun and "floating" restaurant in Walt Disney's Lake Buena Vista is Fulton's Crab House designed by Marve Cooper Design of Chicago. It makes a brilliant statement at night as it is illluminated by thousands of bulbs that out-line the different levels of the boat and the neon glow from the signage on top.

B

C

D

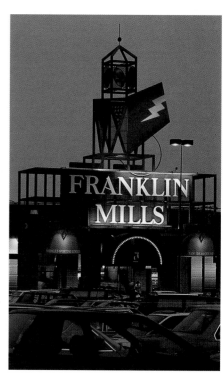

ENTERTAINMENT CENTERS & MALLS

·Beacons and signposts: beckon shoppers, entertainment seekers and diners off the highways and into these mammoth conglomerates of shops, restaurants, and amusements. Facades aglow with colored tints and entrance ways soaring high with metal and g lass superstructures all lit up with graphics, logos and signage for the malls or entertainment centers are the "sirens" that call to and finally ensnare the "lotus eaters" of the late 20th century.

Ontario Mills, Ontario, CA
Design: Glynn Brown Design,
Kansas City, MO

Broward Mall, Broward, FL
Design: FRCH, New York, NY

The Great Mall of the Bay Area,
Milpitas, CA
Design: FRCH, New York, NY

Janss Marketplace
Design: RTKL Assoc.,
Baltimore, MD
Photography: Deave Whitcomb

Franklin Mills, Greater
Philadelphia, PA

C

DOWNTOWN DEPARTMENT STORES

Department stores make striking exclamation points in the downtown streetscapes at night when the multi-level structures are all lit up. Some, like Garcez in Rio (A) and Harrads (B) in London are outlined with thousands of clear incandescent bulbs while others step out in full glory thanks to giant floodlights on neighboring buildings or downlights and uplights that are architecturally incorporated into the building's design.

Samartaine's (C) art deco facade glows as it stands beside the Seine in Paris. Sogo's

store in Taichung, Taiwan (D), designed by the Pavlik Design Group of Ft. Lauderdale, is eerily illuminated with cool halides and The Walker Group/CNI's Iwataya department store complex (E) in Fukuoka, Japan strongly states its presence in the commercial streetscape of this island city.

Brennan Beer Gorman Architect of New York used light to subtly accentuate the art deco architecture of the renovated Bullock's building in downtown Los Angeles (F).

A

B

E

F

D

F

A

B

C

DOWNTOWN

The sun goes down but the retail scene comes alive. The illuminated display window finally get to do their thing without battling the daylight outside. Colors become richer and more brilliant under the artificial light. With Big Box stores and nationally advertised brand name manufacturers making bigger and bigger shows in the downtown retail streets, is it any surprise that they also dominate the nightscapes of the city. Here are some examples culled for N.Y., Chicago and Tokyo.

A: Nike, E. 57th St., New York, NY

B: Warner Bros., Fifth Ave. & E. 57th St.,
New York, NY
Jon Greenberg Assoc.

C: Cole Haan, Madison Ave., New York, NY
Forbes Shea Architects

D: LaCoste, Madison Ave., New York, NY
Forbes Shea Architects
Wade Zimmerman, Photographer

E: Sulka, Oak St., Chicago, IL
Robert Young Assoc.

F: Tiffany's, Tokyo, Japan
Robert Young Assoc.

G: Hyundai, Chonho, Seoul, Korea
Pavlik Design Team

G

D

E

PICCADILLY CIRCUS

LONDON, ENGLAND

The Broadway and Times Square of London could well be the famous Piccadilly Circus and its world recognized fountain topped by Hermes racing off to make the curtain at a theater just up the street. The giant commercial signboards with their changing graphics and color and light patterns make this neighborhood come alive after sunset.

Usually the fountain and the streets that surround it are clogged with natives and tourists alike rushing to a cinema, a noted theme restaurant, the theater, fast food operations, game arcades, or just to the souvenir shops that remain open way into the night they all take advantage of the alluring quality of the bright lights of Piccadilly Circus.